UPDATED EDITION

SOLO PIANO
OPTIONAL CELLO

# THE PIANO (

MW00800522

Visit The Piano Guys at: **thepianoguys.com**

ISBN 978-1-4803-4310-8

Visit Hal Leonard Online at
**www.halleonard.com**

Contact us:
**Hal Leonard**
7777 West Bluemound Road
Milwaukee, WI 53213
Email: info@halleonard.com

In Europe, contact:
**Hal Leonard Europe Limited**
42 Wigmore Street
Marylebone, London, W1U 2RN
Email: info@halleonardeurope.com

In Australia, contact:
**Hal Leonard Australia Pty. Ltd.**
4 Lentara Court
Cheltenham, Victoria, 3192 Australia
Email: info@halleonard.com.au

*As performed by The Piano Guys*

# ALL OF ME

By JON SCHMIDT

**Freely, like a Fanfare**

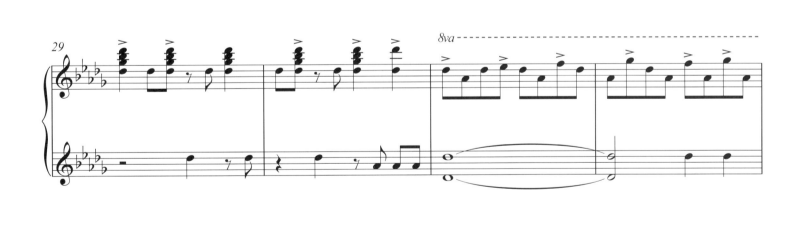

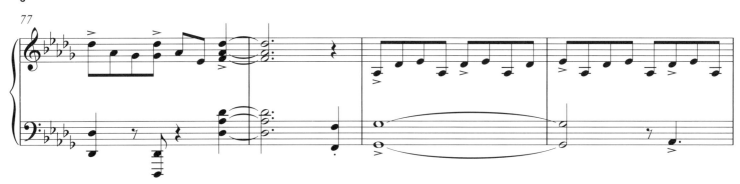

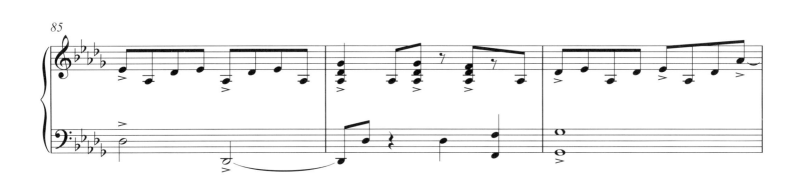

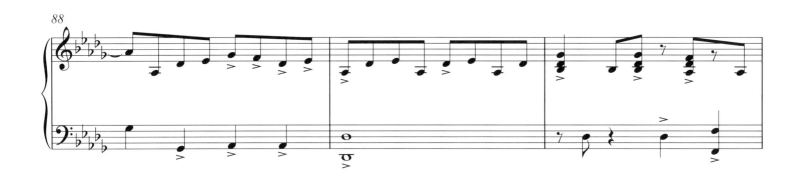

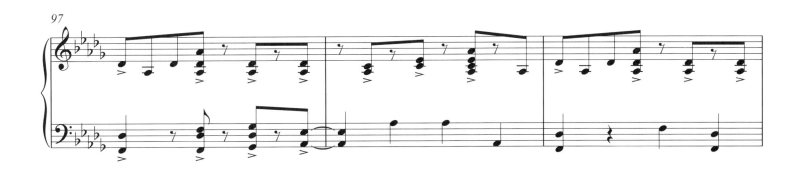

*Use left forearm across general area (elbow pointed left).*
  *- Lift wrist so that left hand doesn't strike any notes.*
  *- Not overly loud.*

*Or you can select any portion of the chord to play with your fingers,*
*if playing with your arm takes you too far out of your comfort zone.*

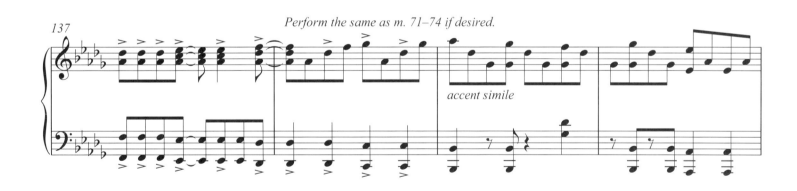

Perform the same as m. 71–74 if desired.

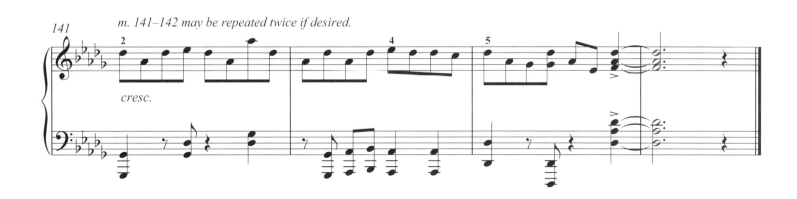

m. 141–142 may be repeated twice if desired.

*As performed by The Piano Guys*

# ARWEN'S VIGIL

By JON SCHMIDT,
STEVEN SHARP NELSON
and AL VAN DER BEEK

*No pedal lift here.*

Let ring as long as desired
with half pedal.

*As performed by The Piano Guys*

# BEGIN AGAIN
## Inspired by J.S. Bach's Cantata No. 208, *Sheep May Safely Graze*

Words and Music by
TAYLOR SWIFT
Arranged by Al van der Beek,
Jon Schmidt and Steven Sharp Nelson

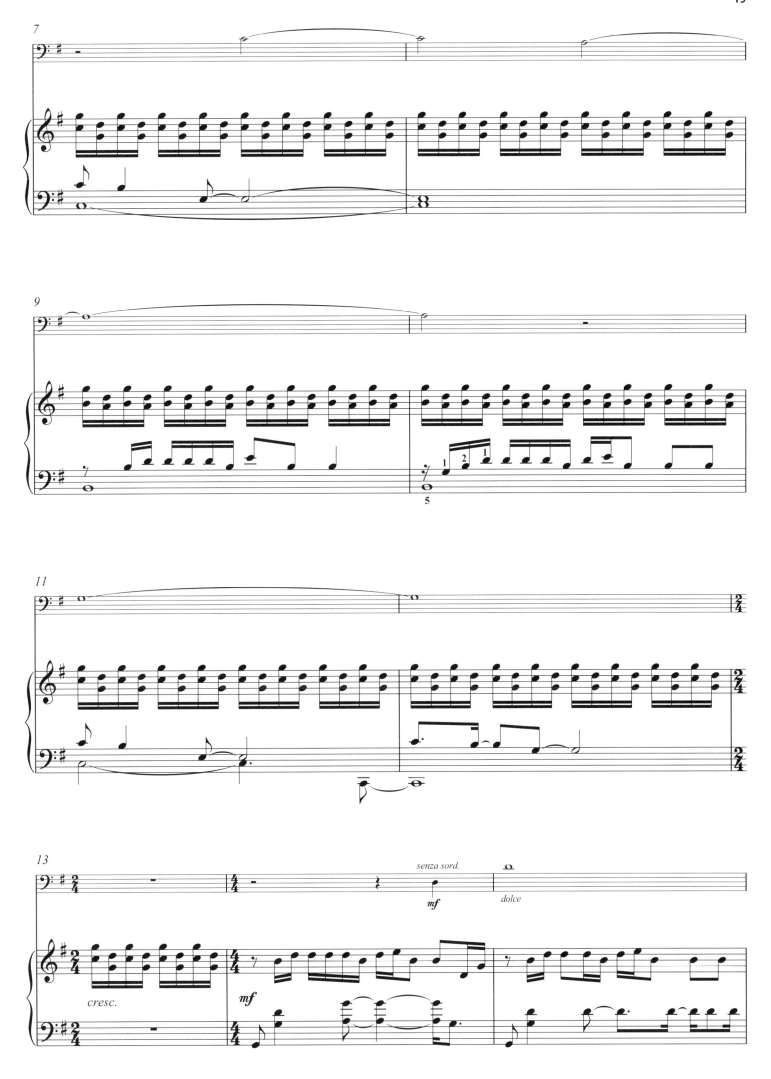

*Bring out left hand melody*

*Small hand: omit or delay top note of chord.*

*pedal lift*

*As performed by The Piano Guys*

# BRING HIM HOME
## from LES MISÉRABLES

Music by CLAUDE-MICHEL SCHÖNBERG
Lyrics by HERBERT KRETZMER and ALAIN BOUBLIL
Arranged by Al van der Beek,
Jon Schmidt and Steven Sharp Nelson

Small hand: delay top note.

*As performed by The Piano Guys*

# CAN'T HELP FALLING IN LOVE

Words and Music by GEORGE DAVID WEISS,
HUGO PERETTI and LUIGI CREATORE
Arranged by Jon Schmidt

**Circumambulatively** (♩ = 132-148)

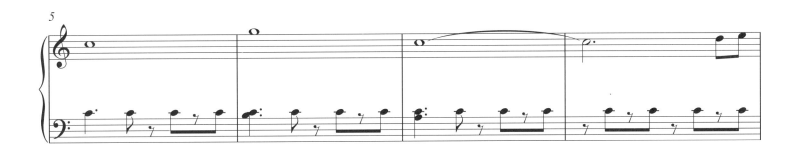

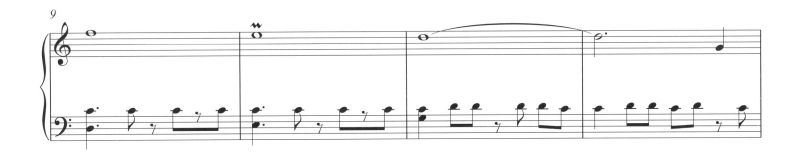

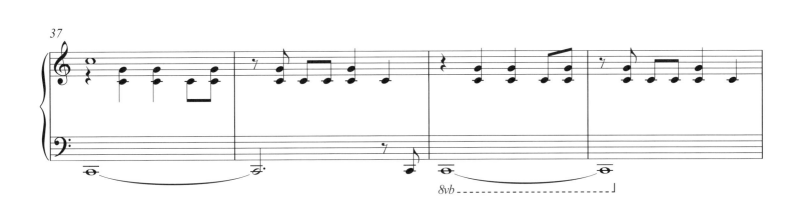

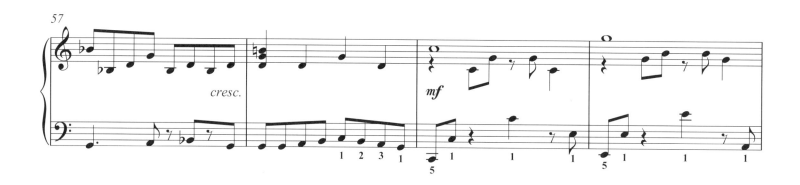

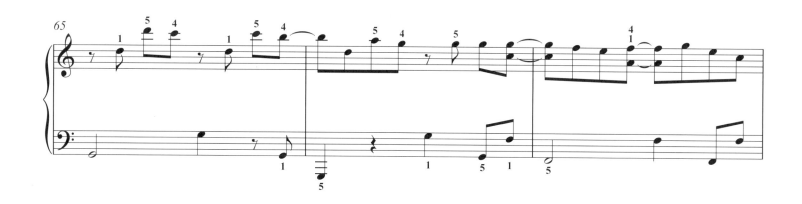

Optional double
trill on C♯ and E.

**Freely**

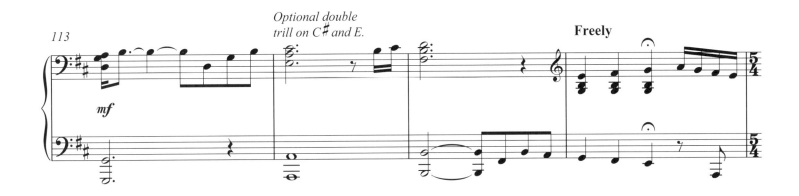

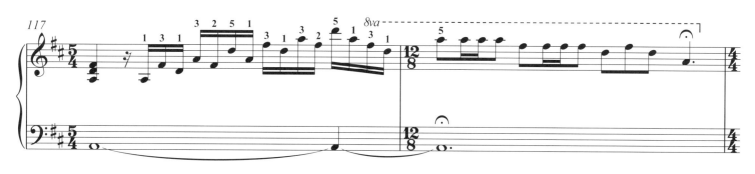

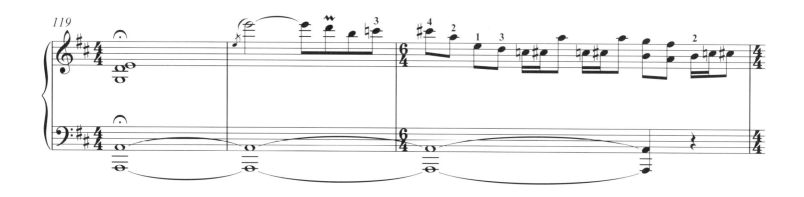

Optional skip to m. 127.

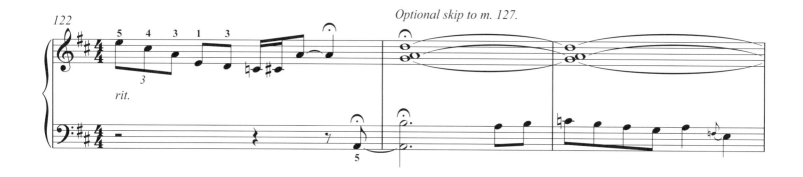

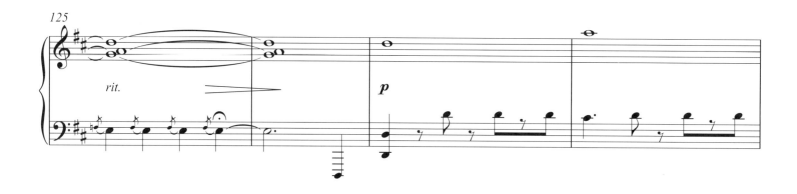

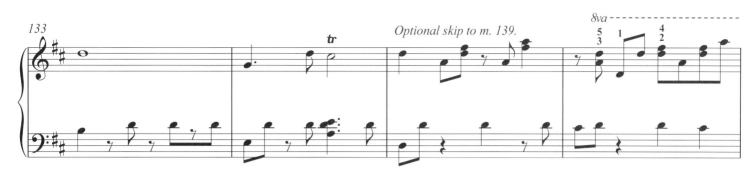

Optional skip to m. 139.

cresc.

cresc.

rit.

*As performed by The Piano Guys*

# HOME

### Inspired by "Going Home," *Largo* melody from Dvořák's *New World Symphony*

Words and Music by GREG HOLDEN
and DREW PEARSON
Arranged by AL VAN DER BEEK,
JON SCHMIDT and STEVEN SHARP NELSON

small hand delay C

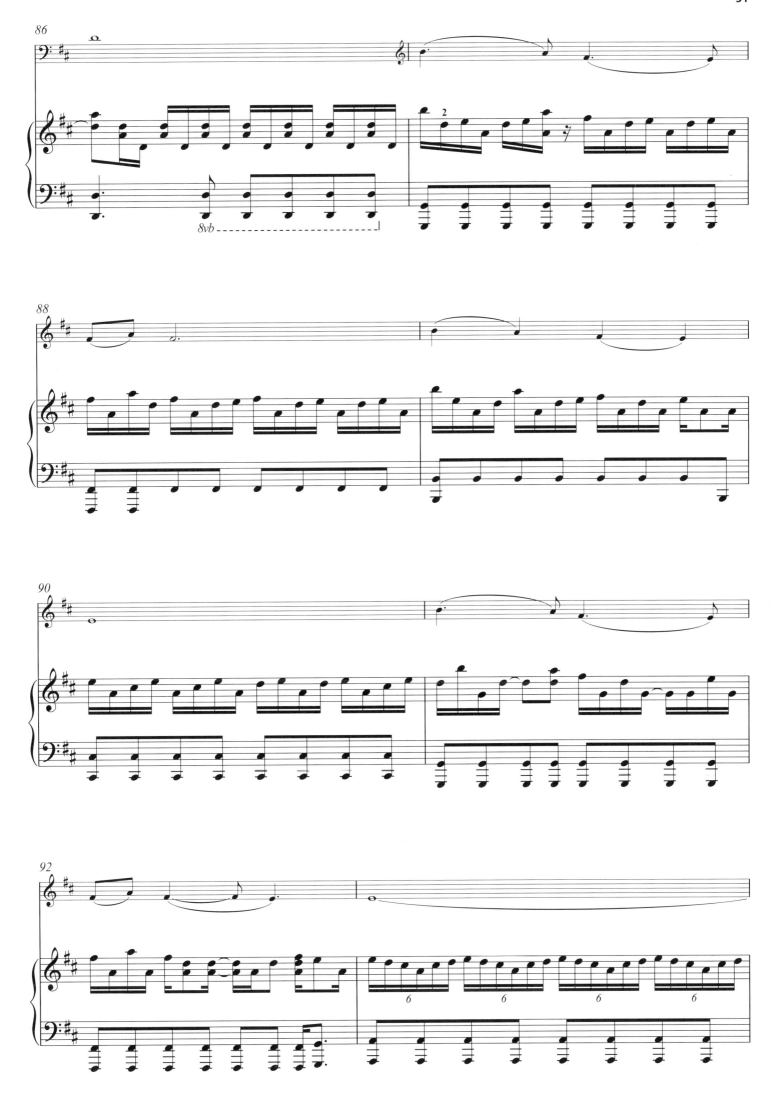

52

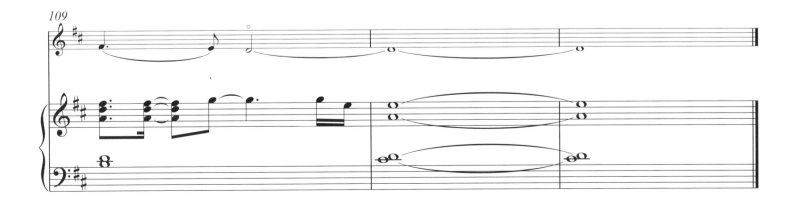

*As performed by The Piano Guys*

# JUST THE WAY YOU ARE

Words and Music by BRUNO MARS,
ARI LEVINE, PHILIP LAWRENCE,
KHARI CAIN and KHALIL WALTON
Arranged by Jon Schmidt,
Al van der Beek and Steven Sharp Nelson

Moderately, freely (♩ = 100)

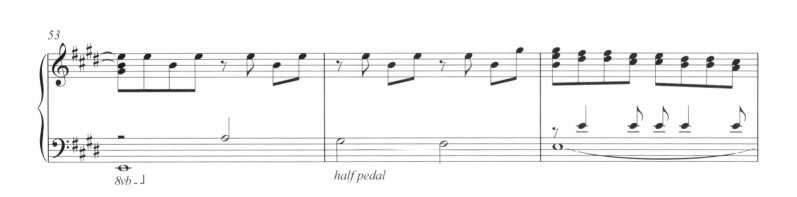

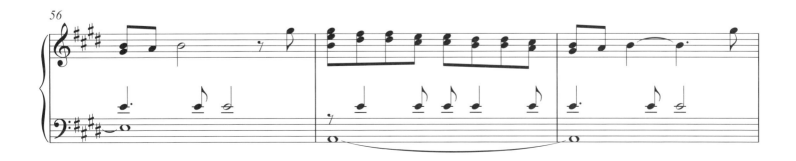

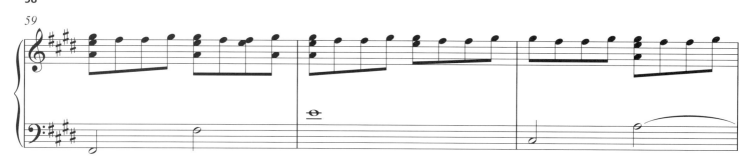

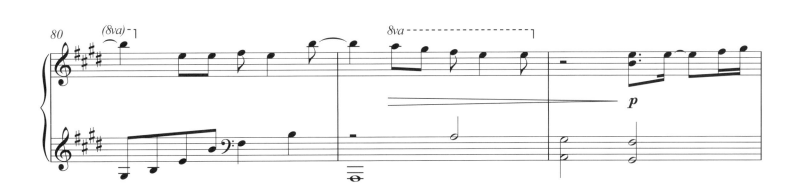

*As performed by The Piano Guys*

# A THOUSAND YEARS

## from the Summit Entertainment film THE TWILIGHT SAGA: BREAKING DAWN - PART 1

Words and Music by DAVID HODGES
and CHRISTINA PERRI
Arranged by Jon Schmidt,
Al van der Beek and Steven Sharp Nelson

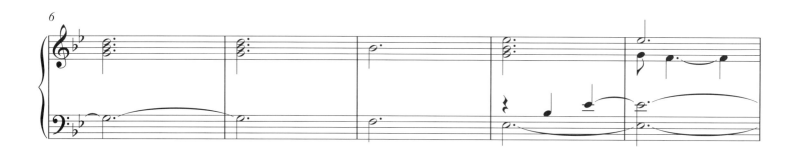

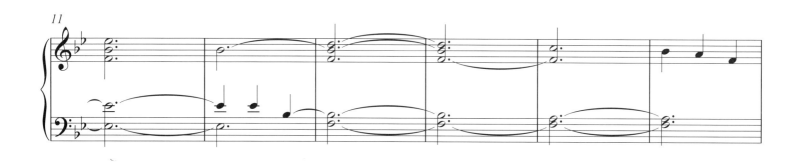

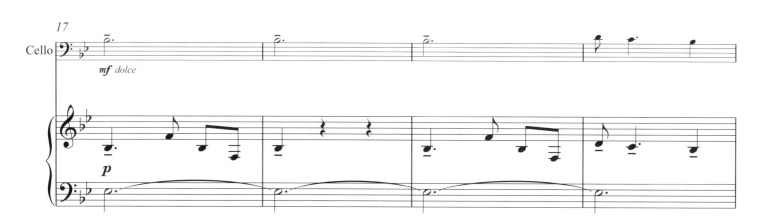

*Bring out melody*

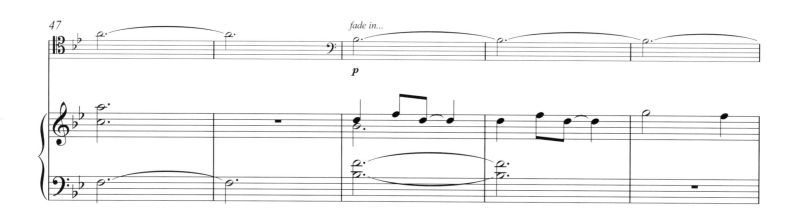

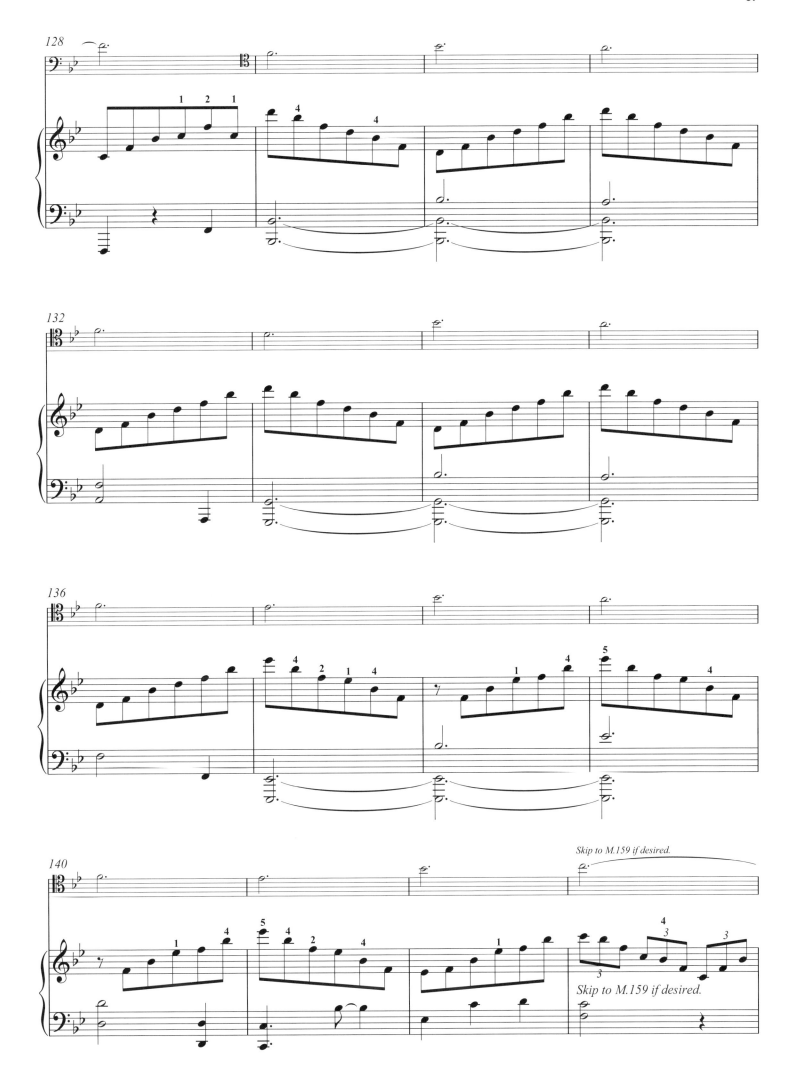

Skip to M.159 if desired.

Skip to M.159 if desired.

# TWINKLE LULLABY

By JON SCHMIDT

*As performed by The Piano Guys*

# MICHAEL MEETS MOZART

By JON SCHMIDT,
AL VAN DER BEEK and STEVEN SHARP NELSON

**Passionately** (♩ = 182)

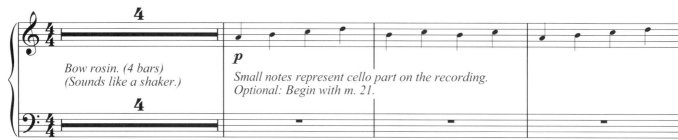

*Bow rosin. (4 bars)*
*(Sounds like a shaker.)*

*p*

*Small notes represent cello part on the recording.*
*Optional: Begin with m. 21.*

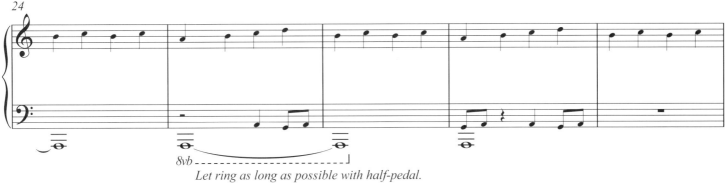

*Let ring as long as possible with half-pedal.*

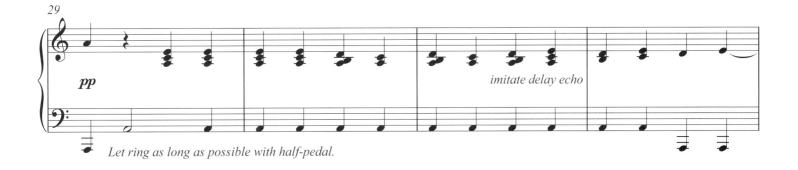

*pp*

*imitate delay echo*

*Let ring as long as possible with half-pedal.*

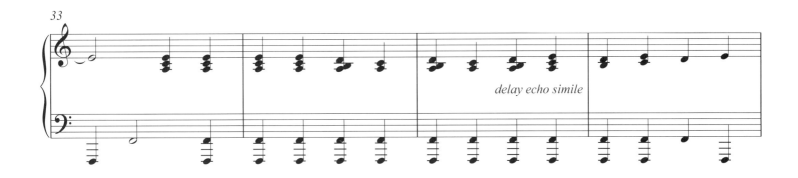

*delay echo simile*

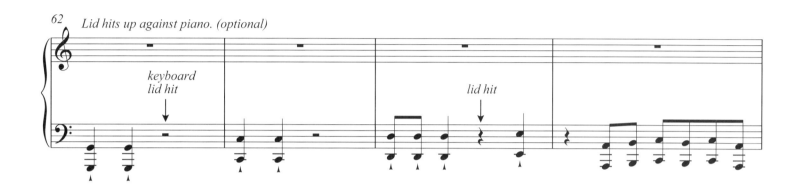

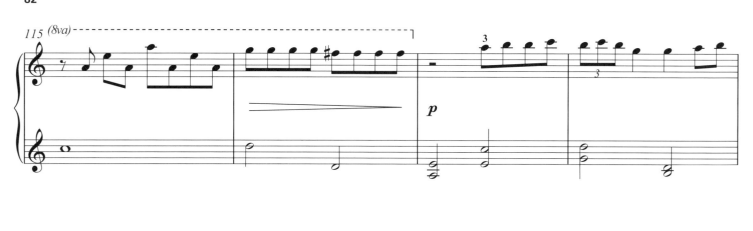

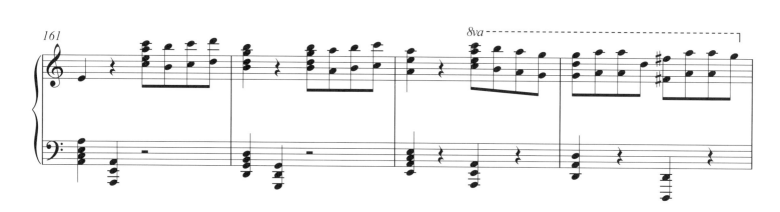

Skip to m. 209 if desired.

R.H. 8va to the end.

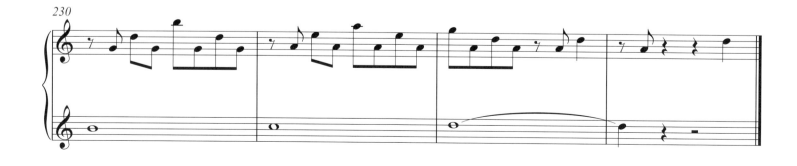